Mrs.
EVERYTHING

Mrs. EVERYTHING

BECOMING THE
Wife, Girlfriend & Mistress

Raymond Sharp, M.Ed.

Copyright: 2020

All Rights Reserved

Printed in the United States of America

ISBN-13: 978-1-7353516-1-2

BOOK RAYMOND SHARP FOR YOUR NEXT CONFERENCE, WORKSHOP OR SEMINAR. SEND YOUR REQUEST TO SHARPSEMINARS@GMAIL.COM.

Contents

Disclaimer 7

Introduction 11

One: The Issue with Men 15

Two: Becoming the Wife, Girlfriend and Mistress .. 27

Three: The Relationship Detox 39

Four: Understanding Your Competition 57

Five: Becoming a Safe Space 65

Six: How to Overcome Fear & Temptation 73

Seven: Epilogue: The Power of Choice 85

Disclaimer

Please Read and Consider

Some of the examples and allusions used may seem to be redundant clichés and generalizations. While some situations discussed may seem far-fetched, they are real-life examples gained from personal and professional relationships as well as advisement sessions. You will be exposed to a perspective that may be the opposite of your personal experiences. If the situations and scenarios presented in this book are not your challenges, consider the individuals close to you dealing with challenges that you find easy to scoff at. If nothing else, use this as a reference for what you cannot relate to. Many believe "it" will not happen to them, until "it" does.

Hoc quaerere…In this, find yourself.

Introduction

"You may kiss the bride!" These are the words my pastor joyfully declared once my wedding vows were exchanged. I was nervous and then filled with peace as I kissed my wife. Excitement overcame me as cheers erupted among those in attendance for our nuptials. I was anxious this time around. It was my second marriage; I knew all about beginnings. My question was, how would things end with my new wife? Would we last? I'm sure many people have the same questions at this very moment for various reasons. My thinking was driven by the failure of a previous marriage. My ex-wife and I had experienced a number of challenges we were not able to overcome; chief among them were trust, communication and a misunderstanding of our needs. To further complicate the challenges of my first marriage, we had to overcome the preconceived notions of her failed previous marriage and our age difference. I thought I was mature, but I didn't understand the magnitude of my responsibilities as a husband. I do not believe my ex-wife and I looked through the same lens, and that started an avalanche that ultimately ended our marriage.

Fortunately, this does not have to be your story. I'd like to give you insight into what a man thinks about relationships and how a woman can prevent potential marital pitfalls. I will be as honest as possible and speak from a practical perspective. Most of all, I want to debunk some myths about men; we care about what women think; we also have difficulty expressing our emotions and needs.

After the failure of my first marriage, I wanted to give my friends insight into how marriage can work and the mistakes and missteps I made. Those who listened have successful marriages; those who didn't listen are divorced, separated or struggling to find peace in their homes. I sincerely hope you will benefit from my error and correction, as I am very happily married, with children. I do not like that I was a lab rat with my first marriage, but I learned from my mistakes and those of my ex-wife. I am determined that others will not repeat our shortfalls. Now that I have moved on and matured, I am looking forward to growing with my wife. She keeps me on my toes and is the principal reason I can confidently write this book. If women would humor me, men pay attention, and

Introduction

married couples decide to patiently work on the concerns and issues in their marriage, then I am confident every man can see his wife as his girlfriend and his mistress. There is no reason to look outside of marriage for your needs. You must look from the premise that your spouse has everything they need. Accept your role and responsibility in bringing out the best in your spouse.

One

The Issue with Men

Everything a man needs for marital bliss and success in life can be found in his wife. However, some men are unknowledgeable about how to seek and reap the benefits of having a well-prepared spouse. Some men don't trust themselves beyond superficial, self-imposed limitations. Men must be honest. Instead, they find ways around dealing with how they truly think and feel with their wives. Again, all a man has to do is trust the woman he chose to marry. Instead, some men live unstable lives focused on what they can get away with versus coming clean with their wives. Along the way, wives pick up cues that something is wrong. Most wives have genuine concern for their husbands; they want to jump in to help. When the path forward to a solution isn't evident, some women become even more committed to getting to the bottom of the issue. The opposite reaction, unfortunately, can be a husband who goes deeper into hiding his issues and addressing them elsewhere.

Men need to develop more of a keen understanding of their wives and the perceived nagging and complaining we often blame our wives for. In many cases, a wife is making an honest attempt to improve her husband by pointing out opportunities that could make a difference or deficiencies that could be a detriment to his personal or professional growth. The opposition men face in marriage doesn't come from their wives; it comes from their inability to value what their wives can contribute to their lives. When a man rejects his wife's assistance, he is cutting off a main function of a wife, which is to help him meet the goals and objectives in his life.

A man is responsible for bringing out everything he needs in his wife. Your wife is designed to be edified, honored and respected and to flourish under any condition. Women flourish best when they are secure in their role and confident in the level of commitment from their husbands. It is very important to women that men give them insight into how they fit into their future, and it is equally important for men to convey how women fit into getting them to their goals. Women, by nature, are supportive and want to know they have a place to add value to men's lives. Due to a lack of positive role models in spousal relationships throughout their lives, most men do not have an example of how to correctly relate to their spouses. In some cases, the example displayed was poor and leaves a false sense of reality in regard to the treatment and role of women in marriage. I loved my father, but I never considered him to be an example of what a man or a husband ought to be. My siblings and I grew up with our father in the home; however, I was aware that he cheated on my mom, failed to keep employment because of an alcohol addiction and was prone to abusive behavior toward his family. My mother saved me and my image of what it meant to be a man. My mother always reminded me to respect my father, but she also told my brothers and me not to model his behavior. I can remember my mother telling me, "Men don't handle business like that. This is how you are supposed to talk to your wife. Men take the time to get their affairs in order." With my mother's voice echoing in my mind, I continued to seek a male role model beyond my father. Like many other young men, I looked up to men in my community. I can say that I have been equally disappointed with what has been uncovered about some of my role models. Of the men I looked to for guidance within a span of 15 years, two tried to sleep with someone I was in a relationship with, another maintained long affairs with multiple women while he was married, one maintained down-low relationships with men, and another abandoned his children. To my surprise, I was totally blown away by all of these developments, but I was actually happy to learn the truth so I could find someone who was living truthfully and ethically, not shuffle behind poor examples while assuming the best.

I am thankful for my mother's guidance in this process because I have friends and colleagues who were stuck in the images and disappointments of their pasts. Dangerously, when faced with a challenge, most people fall back on memories of others in similar situations and regurgitate what they saw or experienced. While most say they would never do or say _____ (you can fill in the blank), you will find them doing that very thing. Men have not seen examples of how to express their feelings without arguing. They don't know how to clearly communicate their emotions without becoming physical; they don't know how to be transparent without fear of ridicule and rejection. The inability of our grandfathers, fathers, and uncles to fight through their silence and yield control of their emotions to their spouses while focusing only on keeping them happy without expressing their thoughts led these men to seek an outlet outside of the home. Over time, this effect has turned from private, unspoken indiscretions to a badge of honor proving one's manhood. Unfortunately, we live in a time when married men know more people who are divorced and unfaithful than men who are happily married and faithful to their wives.

The previous statement, although not scientific, can be easily surmised. Take about ten minutes to recall at least ten men who are married. Of the ten, how many aren't cheating and are happily married? What's more interesting are the societal pressures that have eased on men in regard to keeping a standard of faithfulness in marriage. Some of the males that men look to for guidance, such as pastors, civic leaders and educators, are becoming exposed for having illegitimate children, extramarital affairs and even participating in pedophilia. In regard to men and marriage, the question moves from how could he cheat on his wife to how long before he is exposed? The perceived standard of marital vows seems to mean less, and the expectation to take advantage of what is available outside a man's home seems to be the norm.

What must men do to keep their sanity, vows and their wives in a posture to give them everything they need? My answer is simple, yet complex. Men must decide to reject abandoning their responsibilities and commitments. Men must be resolute in remaining true to their commitments and work through the ease of low expectations. I believe without a doubt in my mind that women are designed to meet every social, emotional, physical, sexual and spiritual need of a man. There's no need for multiple women when one will suffice. If there is a lack of fulfillment in a man's marriage, then it is up to him to awaken it in his spouse. Too many men are living incomplete lives in their relationships. Men are incomplete not because of their spouses, but due to their inability to communicate and relate their heart to their spouses. The result is men seeking fulfillment outside of their relationships in women who pose a threat to the very institution of marriage they committed to. It is my opinion that every man wants a girlfriend and a mistress in addition to his spouse. A man doesn't want a girlfriend and mistress any more than he wants to communicate and relate to his wife in ways he sees as closed off. I intend to give insight into finding these in your spouse and identify the foolishness of being fulfilled outside of the home.

A married man who wants a mistress in his wife cannot forget what is enticing about a mistress. A mistress is usually visually appealing; her hair, nails and attire are usually on par with the latest fashion, and she's great physical shape. Men cut their wives from the mistress status unknowingly because of life and responsibilities. Men shift their attention, at times, to providing for their homes instead of providing for their needs. Yes, the man is a provider for the home, but he cannot forget to make sure his wife is in a position to fully provide everything he needs. As a result, men remove the resources from the homes for their wives to be spontaneous, cutting the budget for sexy lingerie, exotic trips, and maintenance for their wives. Men say there's a budget for these things or that their wives are free to take care of these on their own, but how many actually plan and make allowances in their budgets? By not making allowances, the man comes to believe that he isn't a priority and will seek his mistress outside of the home. A husband must rid his wife of distractions that will prohibit her from facilitating the role of mistress in his marriage. A mistress is normally single, has no children and has extra time on her hands. I would advise men to send the kids to a babysitter for an evening, occasionally hire someone to clean the house, and even cook so their wives can be well rested and attentive to their needs.

Men must sacrifice for their homes. It costs to have what is desirable. If you desire to have a successful business, you must make an investment, whether it's time, resources or money. Money and penny-pinching boggle me when it comes to men and their wives. Most men who seek mistresses will not give their wives money for various reasons, but are willing to spend money on hotels, meals and trips with their mistresses. As crazy as it sounds, one way for men to remain happy at home is to turn the tables on their thoughts. Thoughts are the cancer eroding a man's ability to remain stable and in the arms of his wife. Instead of giving in to the "what if's" and "what I could get from another woman," men need to turn their thoughts to their wives. If a man thinks a woman who isn't his wife is attractive, then he needs to tell his wife she is attractive. If a man is tempted to steal some time for a lunchtime rendezvous with another woman, then he should immediately plan a romantic lunch with his wife. Eventually, his thoughts will begin to turn to his spouse instead of the temptation that lurks at every corner. The most powerful deterrent against the mistress who is not in the home is the mistress at home.

Because of societal pressures, men marry for various reasons unrelated to the fulfillment of their destiny and purpose. Some men marry because of convenience. Some men have become selfish leeches who are looking for women who remind them of their mothers more than a spouse who will hold them accountable and have high expectations for them. I believe this is due in part, again, to a lack of positive examples of men functioning in the role of husbands in their homes and communities. What some men now see growing up, due to a lack of fathers in the home, is a relationship with their mother where she is seen as both a nurturer and a provider. Some men seek to mirror this role perception as they seek romantic and spousal relationships. Some men no longer seek wives who are a reincarnation of their mothers because they don't know what a wife looks like. In other words, men become situational proposers to their girlfriends for reasons such as pregnancy, length of the relationship, social acceptance, a climb in social status, and finances. Men understand that certain employment opportunities will not be available to them unless they are married, because in some circles, marriage is a sign of stability and commitment. What is the solution? Selfishness must be completely disregarded. Any relationship that is not predicated on finding ways to improve one another is dangerous and should be avoided. Any gain that is not connected to seeing the value in an individual above what they provide access to should be avoided as well.

It is difficult to alter your mind once it has conformed to a certain behavior. What's more interesting is that it is usually easier to see the issue in someone else rather than yourself. I challenge every man to imagine his wife's best friend. Also imagine she has a son who was raised in a single-parent home his entire life. This young man sees his father twice a year, on his birthday and at Christmas dinner, but he receives child support every month on time. He loves his mother and is very close to her. He eventually goes to college, graduates, and secures employment. He begins a relationship with a woman, and it seems more like a maternal relationship than a romantic relationship. When he talks about her, he seems drawn to how she can provide for him more than anything else. He makes statements like, "With what she makes, we can..." or "She can take care of me." More than consulting her about his important decisions, he asks her permission. He is unable to separate and show love for her from what she is able to do for him. This does not sound like a healthy relationship that is headed for long-term success, but this is what a great number of men have in their minds concerning relationships and marriage. I have two questions for men: "How well could you identify with this young man?" and, "Are you this young man?" I challenge every man to search his feelings and emotions to find the truth about himself. Ladies, these are platforms from which you can ask questions. My advice would be to come from a position of wanting to understand motivations, not criticism.

 Even though I experienced negative examples in my life, I knew it was the wrong behavior and did not allow what I saw to give me an excuse to behave contrary to what I knew was right. In my heart, I felt differently about everything I saw and experienced. I believe a lot of men have the same revelation but refuse to respond to the correct impulses. Why? Because changing involves work and challenges the foundation upon which a great deal of ideals and beliefs are based. No one wants to admit that there are issues with their foundation, but once these issues are addressed, you can become more stable and aware of other issues that are more pressing and need attention. Ladies, take the time to understand that the challenges men face may be deeply rooted. These challenges can be overcome, but it may take time.

Two

Becoming the Wife, Girlfriend and Mistress

When a man thinks about a mistress, he thinks about a mysterious woman who enflames his passion. His best friend may not even know about this woman, but he's eager to steal away any time he can with her. The mistress knows how to bring out the passion in him. She is dangerous, adventurous, and never says no. The mistress is accommodating and attentive. A man does not need to speak as much as use his posture and his eyes to move her into action. A mistress knows her position, but carries respect because she is aware of the sensitivity of their arrangement. A mistress knows how to get to the point, understands her purpose and is ready to fulfill her role once she is called upon. No talking, no questions; she knows exactly what she needs to do, accomplishes her task, and goes along with her life like nothing happened.

Every wife needs to be a mistress to her husband. Marriage needs to be fresh and vivacious, and women have the ability to breathe new life into their marriages. The most effective mistress meets a need that is not being addressed. Analyze your husband, and ask, "What does my husband need? What is he lacking in our relationship?" Answering these questions will help close the doors to other women. The most important aspect of these questions is not only asking them, it is pouncing in response. I can honestly say that it is difficult for me to think about another woman when my wife is meeting all of my needs. My wife is diligent in performing maintenance on our marriage to make sure there are no open doors for another woman to come in. My wife is diligent as asking simple and open-ended questions that will not yield a yes or no answer. My wife's questions are not an interrogation; they're just a diagnostic to make sure everything is going well and there are not any cracks in our marriage.

A misconception about a mistress is that sex is the lure for a man to stray. Women would be surprised to find that a lot of men have fallen victim to a mistress through conversation, compliments from another woman or by a woman saying she respects the man that he is. The dangerous thing about a mistress is that a man can begin to care for her. Once a man starts to care for his mistress, he places false hope in something that was never meant to be permanent. A temporary fix can cause a laundry list of issues for a marriage. Regardless of what people may say or think, a wife can keep her husband in suspense. It helps when a woman is not predictable. By no means am I advocating for a wife to mislead her husband, lie to him or use deceitful tactics. However, use what you know about your husband to lure him; find ways to become mysterious and desirable.

 A woman can keep her husband on his toes with subtle things. If your husband likes to play golf, take the liberty of scheduling a golf outing. If your husband likes videogames, purchase him a gift card or pre-order the game he wants. If your husband works on his feet all day, surprise him with a foot massage occasionally. A man will not request these things, but trust me, he appreciates them all. A wife must be willing to blow her husband's mind. Consider the mistress; she looks forward to her encounter with another woman's husband just to show him how much she appreciates him. Should you, as his wife, be the object of his affection and his heart's desire? So, what do you do if you know your husband is currently lost to the attention of a mistress? First, look at yourself and ask, "If I was my husband, what wouldn't I like about me?" In other words, "What am I doing to turn him off?"

Men stray when they have issues that are not easy to discuss or express. Men are lost to mistresses because of accessibility. Even in the event of an indiscretion, some men want to tell the truth but are afraid of the wrath and consequences that accompany their admission. This is not the case for men who are habitual and willful cheaters. However, there are men who know they've made mistakes. They want to improve the relationship with their wives, but they don't know how to begin the conversation. More than what a man wants to hear is what he wants to see and know. A man wants to know that his wife is ready to receive him back. Most men can admit when they're wrong and want to change their current state, but they want their wives to be open to hearing what they have to say. One of the most sensitive times in the process is placing blame. A husband will blame his wife for what she didn't do, and a wife will blame her husband for not communicating, and the list can go on and on. What a woman needs to do is take time to find the correct words for a difficult conversation. A man already knows the hurt he caused, but can work on establishing trust and a new beginning. Although trust was broken, love, forgiveness, and restoration must be the foundation of discussing challenging issues. If you do not go into the situation with this approach, bitterness, hatred and revenge will be the result. New ground rules must be set establishing boundaries for the marriage. The ground rules must include open conversation and a willingness to give your spouse a clean slate so you both can heal and move forward. This can be difficult; patience is a definite requirement.

Patience is a dirty word for a lot of people. Patience, however, helps move things along in a relationship. A misconception of patience is that it involves time, which is completely untrue. Patience has everything to do with how one deals with a process. The Merriam-Webster Dictionary defines patience as "the act of bearing pains or trials calmly or without complaint." As you can see, it has nothing to do with time but everything to do with your attitude. You must decide how you will overcome situations that negatively affect you in a relationship. While you must have conversations about negative situations, you can still be graceful in the interaction. Patience is something a mistress understands and embraces. If a woman wants to keep her spouse, she must take on the role of a mistress who doesn't judge and offers solutions to the challenges of her lover. A woman must also make sure she is not robbing her husband of her ability to be a mistress to him by fulfilling the role for another man. A wife's energy is best suited for her husband. It's simply crazy to complain about a need one is not able to fulfill for the sole reason one is doing it for another. This is true about the role of a girlfriend in one's marriage.

When a man thinks about a girlfriend, he thinks about someone he calls upon to share a great time. There is quality conversation, and she is worth the time and resources. The girlfriend is well-respected and regarded as someone in whom a man has placed some value. A man develops a trust in his girlfriend, but he is still feeling her out to make sure she is as advertised. The girlfriend is reliable and gives a man a sense of assurance; men show off their girlfriends and take pride in their presence. The girlfriend is the heartbeat of a man. Girlfriends are a man's confidence, the source of his smile, and a sanctuary of peace. Men date their girlfriends and develop a friendship that is more personal and involved than the relationship with their mistresses. Men spend time with their girlfriends out of desire, not obligation, which is why courtship is at its best, and men go out of their way to impress and connect with the object of their affection. While wooing a girlfriend, friendship is sparked, communication is kindled, and love is realized. On the other hand, this is one of the most dangerous relationships because of the emotions involved. A man is usually infatuated with his girlfriend because her best is usually exhibited and appreciated. At the same time, her worst is visible, ignored, and silenced, which leads to compromise because a blind eye is turned to details that should alarm men prior to the consideration of marriage. Men aren't considering the pitfalls; everything is cute and funny because they are blinded by attraction and/or lust. Because of the lack of perspective and practical sight, men are forgiving of their girlfriends.

Defining a girlfriend is challenging because perceptions differ. Some men treat their girlfriends like mistresses, while others treat their girlfriends like they are their wives. While expectations in relationships differ, there's a fine line to getting it right without muddling what is needed from a man in a relationship. What men miss in their spouses is the simplicity of getting to know one another while basking in the glow of their presence. Once one enters a marriage, the focus is on so many things – work, finances, kids, chores inside and outside the home, and involvement in one another's outlets. Family and friends tend to get in the way of developing the one thing that matters the most, which is maintaining an open and growing relationship with one another.

    Married men need someone to talk to. If I can offer any advice to women, it is for them to manage the time and events in life so their husbands can see the girlfriend in them. One of the worst things couples can do is get to a point where they put their relationship on cruise control. When a relationship is on cruise control, it creates an opportunity for another person to take control. Women must be alert and not take for granted that everything is going smoothly. A wife must perform maintenance on the relationship and reconnect with her spouse as much as possible. Do not forget that you are the spice that adds flavor to your husband's life. You have the ability to put a smile on his face; one glance from you can make his heart melt.

Never forget that you were first his girlfriend, the apple of his eye, and sense of pride and joy. Just as hard as you worked to get him to feel this way about you, you have to work even harder to maintain it.

Men normally are not drawn to one thing in a woman, but rather a collection of positive attributes of every woman in their life. For example, I wanted my wife to cook like my mother, bake like my great-grandmother, have my back like my sister, and make me laugh like my friend Mary. Men want their wives to be the women of their dreams but have substance as well. Men want their wives to be outgoing but not flirtatious, virtuous but not boring, and compassionate without being a glutton for punishment. In short, men aren't looking for a quality in a spouse, but rather a combination of attributes that will keep them on their toes and looking forward to growing old together. As much as men do not admit it, we like variety, which is why we need to experience all dynamics of relationship stages with our wives. More than anything, men need to know they can trust their wives.

What it boils down to is that if a man cannot trust his wife, nothing else matters; the relationship is dead unless trust can be restored. If a woman wants to be a great wife, she must begin with trust. A man needs to know he can trust his wife with his money, children, and life – especially his children. Just like a farmer seeks the best possible ground to plant his crop, a man looks for a woman who is moral, nurturing, and pleasant to give birth to his children. If a man cannot see a woman as a mother, it will be difficult for him to see her as a wife. I can honestly say that my wife has not disappointed me. She is a woman who loves me unconditionally. My wife is the complete and total package. She is my wife, girlfriend and mistress. This is something that gets lost with some women. Men do not stop needing a woman who is spontaneous, occasionally aggressive and available like a mistress. A man never complains about a woman who is there for him through thick and thin. The key for a successful marriage is being able to discern enough to see how your current ability and personality will translate to your spouse's destiny. My wife has seen me at my worst; I pray that she never sees that side of me again. My wife learned my personality as well as my emotions; she has never deviated from love. Through love and her expression of it to me spiritually, emotionally and physically, I feel compelled and empowered to serve my wife in every way she needs. Where women are off target is with believing that sex is enough to keep a man. Women can use sex as a weapon to hurt, influence, and convince a man they love him. But when sex is not properly combined with love, affection, and conversation, a man can still be left empty.

Do not think for a moment that I'm letting men off the hook. There is one thing every man can do to unlock the ability that women have to fulfill their destinies as power women, spouses and mothers. Women are not properly catapulted because men have an inability to love. Wives can be free from emotional bondage if men know how to properly love and relate love to them. A man must be willing to go through hell for his wife. There is nothing a woman can do to alienate affection from her husband if he is strong and willing to take her to ecstasy in every area of her life. It is a husband's responsibility to make certain his wife does not feel the pain and cruelty of this world. Women are emotional and occasionally respond to their surroundings filtered with fear and concern. Men must bring comfort and peace to the life of their wives so they can move through their day without struggling to feel and experience love on a daily basis.

Three

The Relationship Detox

Successful relationships are all about compromise. At times, it seems some compromise more than others. The fact that some compromise more than others in some areas should not be a mainstay but based upon the seasons in one's relationship. For example, when my wife was pregnant, I knew I had to become more attentive to her physical and emotional needs. Conversely, my wife knew that certain times of the year required me to work from 6 a. m. to 10 p. m. , so the responsibility of the children was squarely on her shoulders. Once the season ended, we shifted to a more normal routine. Similarly, when soldiers are deployed, their spouses pick up the duties and responsibilities of the house until they return. Absence and being unavailable is not a bad thing; it's just required for a period of time. Strong individuals can grasp this fact, but those who are not strong will allow their minds to wander and ask questions such as, "Are they really working late? Who are they spending time with? Why don't they have time for me? I wonder if they are cheating on me. I need to find something on the side because I know they have someone occupying their time." Sadly, the stress of assumptions begins to outweigh the reality of the situation and causes people to act opposite to the reality of their situation.

In any relationship, whether it's professional, social or romantic, one picks up nuanced behaviors and attitudes over time. Typically, the assimilated behaviors and attitudes are essential to the survival of the relationship. Over time, one's mind becomes conditioned to believe that the learned behavior is akin to an overarching relationship and not fine-tuned to a situation or individual. In a presentation on the psychology of relationships, Dr. James M. Graham identified three broad types of attachment styles in regard to relationships. The attachment styles are as follows.

1. Secure: Trusting and Relaxed
2. Anxious-Ambivalent: Nervous and Clingy
3. Avoidant: Suspicious and Withdrawn

In Dr. Graham's research, he noted that only about 60% of individuals are secure and trusting in romantic relationships. The rest, 40% are insecure and are avoidant or anxious about depending on others. Dr. Graham noted that one's attachment styles are learned through experiences in close relationships. You can gather a great deal of insight from understanding your attachment style. You can clearly understand the root of your hang-ups, doubts, fears and, in the best cases, why you are trusting in relationships. It's important to remember that only 60% of people are in secure and trusting romantic relationships. With the national divorce rate at 50%, it is easy to see why; you do not want to be in a relationship with someone who is nervous, clingy, suspicious or withdrawn. This is especially true in marriage when the cause of any negative views of romantic relationships has nothing to do with one's spouse, but previous relationships.

Everyone must go through a relationship detox for the success of their marriage. Humans cling to so much learned behavior that has no relevance in their current relationships. One must take a period of time to rid one's body and mind of old habits, behaviors, expectations, disappointments and personality crutches that exist as a result of previous relationships. In the practical sense, detoxification is of tremendous benefit to your body. Because we don't always know the dangers of what we eat, there can be health issues associated with what is consumed. It is not until we endure a detoxification process that we can see a difference. It has been noted that a detox regimen can help improve organ function, clear one's skin of blemishes, boost energy and may contribute to weight loss. Again, going through a relationship detoxification process is equally important; you may be carrying people, experiences and hurt that are causing your inability to function in their relationship.

The danger of not going through a relationship detox may be putting your marriage at risk. You must come to the realization that your marriage cannot grow unless the conditions are ripe for you to be completely open, honest and free to understand your spouse. If this isn't the case, it will be impossible to maximize the full potential of your spouse in every area of life. Everyone deserves a chance in life and love. One of the greatest challenges to overcome in marriage is disappointment because of preconceived notions and mindsets. If you dig to find the root of disappointment and expectation in your marriage, you may come to the realization that it has nothing to do with your spouse. In actuality, your spouse is not letting you down; your spouse has not been given the opportunity to experience you in your purest form. In particular, there are four areas to detox from previous relationships. You must undergo emotional, physical, personality, and spiritual detoxification.

Emotional Detox

Memories of past hurt often do not leave easily. In some instances, painful memories define and reshape your views on life and relationships. However, you should never hold someone accountable for another's mistakes. If you've experienced hurt, pain and disappointment from a previous relationship, you must let it go for your marriage to have a chance at success. Everyone is different by nature and prone to make mistakes, but not everyone will make the same mistakes they experienced in a previous relationship. It is selfish not to move on from previous relationship disappointments. The worst thing a selfish person can do is get married. When you're married, everything is about the marital unit, not the individual. You must do what is in the best interest of the unit.

No one wants to be in a relationship with an emotionally fragile and unstable individual, especially if their emotional state is based on a relationship they had when they were 18 years old. The process of detoxification from emotional distress and instability requires complete and unconditional forgiveness of the person or persons who are the source of the pain. You must let those who are the source of the pain go, along with the memory of that pain. It's challenging at times, but it is possible. You must focus on what is going well in your marriage and how to relate to your spouse. You must never look at your spouse through the lens of previous relationships and assumptions. You should always make decisions and respond based upon facts, their behavior and asking direct questions. It takes time to build trust, but allow your spouse to build it. Everyone deserves to have a marriage free from false assumptions and unrealistic fear. Give your spouse the opportunity to live with you without doubt; you will find your relationship is more enjoyable. Do not guard yourself from hurt, pain and disappointment that will never come.

Physical Detox: Attraction and Sex

There is a lot to consider with sex and attraction in regard to a physical detox. Physical attraction and sex are the bait that causes people with good intentions toward their spouses to be led away. In the simplest terms, once you're married, you have to let the highs, lows and trauma of all previous sexual encounters die. First I want to mention traumatic sexual experiences. Some people do not look forward to sex because their experiences have been negative. If this is the case, they must share what they have been through with their spouse. There are men and women who feel their spouses don't want to be intimate with them. The issue is not them individually, but stems from an experience where they were taken advantage of in some way. You can help your spouse overcome previous experiences and learn to avoid the triggers that cause them to close themselves off. You must allow yourself to become a source of healing through your spouse's process.

Once you're married, the only sexual experience that matters and counts is the magic that happens with your spouse. If you had amazing sex prior to meeting your spouse, remember why the sex was amazing. For some, it was due to a combination of physical, emotional and mental connections with an individual more than it was the actual sex itself, and for others, it was just great sex. You are well able and capable of having even better experiences if you are willing to put time, effort and thought into how you connect with your spouse.

You should stop all comparisons to previous people when it comes to your spouse. Some people cringe at the thought of being with the same person for the rest of their lives, but it is actually a bonus. You're in a committed, consensual relationship, one which affords the time and opportunity to perfect every need, desire and want. In detoxing from previous sexual experiences, find what your spouse does well and let them work it. Dialogue is important as well. Be prepared to ask and answer difficult questions. Do not take for granted that someone is going to magically figure out what you like. There needs to be an open conversation to make sure your expectations are met and exceeded. Study your spouse, find out what turns them on and what turns them off. Make it a practice to set expectations without relying on your spouse being horny alone. It's selfish to think someone is ready to pounce on you just because you are horny. Some need to be warmed into the mood; find out what gets them going. Sex and lovemaking should be enjoyable for all parties involved. Sex and lovemaking affirm the attraction you have to your spouse; it reconnects you and helps release tension. You shouldn't use your spouse as an instrument of physical masturbation. In other words, your spouse is not an inanimate object; take time to learn what pleases your spouse as you are being physically fulfilled.

Do your best to stay in an attitude of affirmation; nothing can kill a desire in someone who is willing to please their spouse quicker than negativity. Although achieving the ultimate sexual experience with your spouse may be a journey, it is important to give them a chance and not give up on them blowing your mind. It is also important that you develop a sense of sensitivity towards your spouse. It can be confusing if you are rude and then expect the time of your life with her during intimacy. You should practice and prepare for intimacy before the bedroom; remain kind, considerate and in a position of understanding so it will be easy for your spouse to receive you when it is time for your needs to be met. It is also critical to be sensitive if your spouse has any medical issues that make a sexual encounter challenging or painful. Find ways to be creative; don't give up on the encounter altogether. You should always keep a position of understanding; you never know if you will face challenges of your own.

If you have been married for any length of time, there's a great chance your spouse does not have the same physical composition as the wedding day. Just because physical appearance changes, it does not give an individual permission to say they are no longer attractive. As you grow and mature, you will need to redefine beauty, attraction and sexiness. I am attracted to my wife for a myriad of reasons to include physical, emotional, intellectual and spiritual. I will not let weight gain define what I find attractive about my wife. I love who she is. Attraction is a touchy issue in marriage because some people decide to get married for reasons beyond love and attraction. Instead, they marry for comfort, companionship, financial stability and/or social status. Some who get married for the benefits of marriage rather than a connection with an individual can develop an appreciation and attraction to their spouse. You must take time to learn about your spouse, what makes them tick and what you like about them. Prior to getting married, I dated a woman because I liked how pristine her teeth were. I dated someone else because she made me laugh, and another person because I liked how short she was. I liked these women and felt an attraction to them. If I could find an attraction in these small things, I know there is something that can keep drawing you close to your spouse. You must find reasons beyond personal comforts to find what can attract you to your spouse.

Personality Detox

In order to be in the best position to relate to your spouse, there must be a reality check with your personality, which can develop from a need to survive socially, culturally and romantically. Often, individuals project thoughts, motives and ideas that have nothing to do with their worldview. Often, people don't have their own personas; they have adopted a personality amalgamation from celebrities, professional athletes and other pop culture icons. Often, our "personality" is a projection of how we want people to see us instead of who we are. I learned this the hard way. I remember that I looked up to a rapper who shall remain nameless. This rapper mentored me through his music and interviews. I wanted to live and be just like him. In my transformation to be like my "mentor," the most common remark about me was, "Are you okay? You don't sound like yourself." I remember watching "Behind the Music" on VH-1. The moment that hit me was how normal and goofy some of the documentary subjects were. They all had concerns, fears and wanted to be accepted on some level. Ironically, I was seeking to be like an individual who didn't know who he was. Once I focused on finding who I was and conveying it honestly, I met my wife. My wife gave me space to honestly share my opinions about life without judging me; she was just happy to have someone in her life who sought authenticity.

As you detoxify your personality, find your voice, purpose and behavior. Do not express and perpetuate what you want others to believe; be honest and true. In doing so, your spouse will have an opportunity to fall in love with who you are, not what you want your spouse to believe you are. I know this from personal experience. The milestones in my marriage can be marked by occasions where I decided to clearly and honestly communicate my thoughts and emotions to my wife. The first time I met her, we literally talked all night long. I was honest and didn't hold back my true feelings about anything; my wife did the same. I remember feeling that night she was always going to be a part of my life. On another occasion, about a year before we were married, I told my wife I did not want there to be any secrets between us. I started in my childhood and told her every secret I could remember, then I said, "This is who I am and what I have done. Do you still want me?" She said yes, and unprompted, went through the same routine and ended with the same question. My wife and I were drawn to the sincerity in each other. To this day, over 14 years later, we speak openly; nothing is off the table. We both know what to expect from one another; having a grasp of your spouse's personality helps overcome false perceptions and avoids arguments. In a word, it helps peace live in your relationship. When you do not have to refer to a false identity, it is easier for your spouse to get to know who you are.

Spiritual Detox

The spiritual detox is very important to go through. As discussed earlier, people mesh their thoughts and beliefs to mirror those they have an attraction to or want to be with in a relationship. Often in relationships, people get along with their significant other just to keep the peace. In doing so, their core values erode and eventually fade away. If the relationship does not work, they can be left with a worldview and belief system that belonged more to another person than themselves. You must take time to develop a worldview and spiritual identity that resonates with the core of who you are, no matter who you encounter and develop a relationship with. Developing a strong sense of your core values, morals and personal ethics will help center you after a breakup instead of throwing your life in total disarray. This is very important in marriage as well.

Your spirituality, core values, morals and ethics should help you decide who is compatible with the sum of who you are. Compromise in this area will cause conflict to occur internally and externally. Your view of respect for yourself and others is often derived from your spiritual perspective; if you marry an individual who believes differently, conflict is introduced on a personal level that is often seen as offensive. To counter this, you must clearly communicate how you see yourself and what you believe. Give your spouse an opportunity to share her values as well to make certain you're both on the same page.

Before getting married to my wife, we broke up on two occasions because we struggled to find common ground. Breaking up was actually good for us; I had an opportunity to reflect on what I believed and how I saw myself as a citizen of this world. The time off from my relationship helped me realize my beliefs were a hodgepodge of beliefs and ideas a picked up from previous relationships. The time off helped me learn who I was and how I personally felt without filtering it through old emotions and ideologies.

The key to a successful spiritual detox is time and honesty. You must take time to reject what you decided to adopt just to please others and find the true essence of what resonates with your soul. Having time alone to find yourself without interference or improper motives is essential to inner peace and personal growth in a relationship.

Ideally, a relationship detox should take place before marriage. Unfortunately, this is not always the case. You must learn, develop and receive patience with your spouse and yourself to properly reject any old idea, behavior and belief from a previous relationship. You must give your spouse time to develop and evolve; doing so will help improve your marriage, and you'll gain a greater understanding of who your spouse is and what motivates them. Be open in response to the reality that you may need to detox from the pain of the current relationship you're in with your spouse. You must give your spouse space and time to get over old feelings and emotions that may exist because of disappointment, mistreatment and infidelity. Marriage can be a place of trauma. If you want your spouse to commit and recommit to a successful marriage, you must give them attention and help them work through challenges to keep the marriage alive; do not be distant, cold and unforgiving.

No matter where you are, there should always be a detox. The relationship detox should be ongoing; the longer a couple is married, the more they tend to evolve and change. The evolution should be ongoing. At times we have to detox from what used to work. Be it sex, conversations, motivations, children or gifts, you must detox from old ways of doing things to move forward in a healthy manner with your spouse. There is nothing more annoying to me than baby talk. As an educator, I understand the correlation between communication, learning and a child's development. When you refuse to change and detox from old habits, it reminds me of the gibberish and nonsense of baby talk. It has no relevance and meaning, but one believes it is amusing. Get rid of the gibberish and nonsense in your relationship by going through a process of truth and honesty that will allow you to grow and mature personally and along with your significant other. You must always remember there is someone waiting for you not to pay attention to the needs of your spouse. You don't want to easily forfeit your place due to something you can choose to control and adapt to.

Four

Understanding Your Competition

For some women, getting married is the end of the race. It is the culmination of hard work put into looking their best and being on their best behavior. Every moment of past disappointment, pressure to be perfect and paying attention to detail pays off with an engagement and nuptials. Men see the promise of the woman who wowed them; for some women, it's the end of the charade; their guard is dropped and who they really are is exposed. This occurs for many reasons, but chief among them is security; some women do not believe a man will actually leave them for their change in behavior, attitude and lack of commitment to being excellent. Men usually cannot see beyond a fake façade dressed in heels, pearls and layers of makeup; they fail to ask critical questions that will provide insight into a woman's true thoughts and persona. In the end, men are left confused in a committed relationship rethinking their life and the choices they have made. This happened to me ten days after my first marriage; more on that later. I discovered that other friends and colleagues had similar experiences.

In no way am I seeking to bash women and place blame solely on them for men losing interest in them. I want to shine a light on the mental lapses that occur once some women get what they want. I have seen married women who were at their best on their wedding day and at their absolute worst after the honeymoon. Above everything, men value authenticity and reliability. If these qualities cannot be found in their spouse, men would much rather have an affair and hope they will not get caught in order to fill a void than come face-to-face to what they feel is a monster at home. Some wives see women who are visually stunning as competition. Actually, the true competition is women who develop genuine care and concern for their husbands' well-being and are responsive to their needs. This is what draws men to take on mistresses and girlfriends outside of the marriage. In truth, a wife is really in competition with herself not to become selfish and self-centered after a man makes the ultimate commitment to her.

Being married does not give a woman an excuse not to be at her best. There are times of grace in every situation, but a woman's response should never be, "He isn't going anywhere" when questioned about her faults, shortcomings or behavior that may turn off her spouse. Pride is one of the greatest enemies in marriage. Marriage requires daily maintenance; you cannot rest on the work done in previous months, weeks or days. There must be a recommitment to excellence on a daily basis. Are we all excellent every day? No! But the effort needs to be made. Effort can be explained and appreciated, but the effort must be in the areas that make a difference, not what you feel comfortable with only. My wife used to cook dinner for me every day. While I was grateful for it, I did not care about dinner being made when I came home from work. I would much rather come home to a clean home; it helps me relax after a long day. Once we started having children, it was more difficult for my wife to meet that particular need, but she always made an effort to make sure what I initially saw when I came home was clean. Having stair-step children presented its challenges, but I knew my wife's heart and knew she did what she could. I was fine with that. On the other hand, some only focus on what's easy for them and complain that they desire something challenging for them. For some of my friends, their wives cannot cook and refuse to learn or try to learn. My wife struggled in the kitchen when we were first married. Even though cooking is not at the top of my needs, she still wanted to become excellent and asked for recipes, strategies and insight from other women. I love her food, and she is a great cook. Again, her effort was to become excellent in everything she did. Men should put forth this effort as well because it breeds mutual respect and appreciation. There should not be an excuse for what someone cannot do or is not used to when there is so much technology and people offering free self-help tips. In other words, working at being your best can go a long way with your spouse. When I see my wife put effort into improving herself and our marriage, it gives me insight into her heart and passion for me, her goals, and our life together. My wife's effort helps me build trust in her level of commitment to our success.

  One of the most disheartening things a man can hear is no and what his spouse will never do. Hearing words like "no" and "never" from your spouse creates hopelessness and leads to desperate actions. Even if you feel it's something difficult for you, let your spouse know you will try to work on it and encourage them to help come up with a plan for improvement in that area. When some spouses hear words like "no" and "never," it can make them feel their spouses are content with how things are and don't see the value in their needs and/or improving the relationship.

    An area where I absolutely advise telling your spouse no is when it comes to opening the bedroom to other people. Do not give your husband a hall pass, a threesome, orgy or even permission to go to the strip club. If he feels he needs these things because of what he is used to, then direct him to the relationship detox. On the other hand, if he says he is unfulfilled and wants to spice things up, find out what he needs and be that to him. Do not bend under the pressure to change and improve your performance and appearance that you allow other women to occupy his mental pleasure center. In giving in, women place themselves in a position where their husbands are performing an act of vaginal masturbation instead of making love to them. Their focus and attention is on what they want and see from their experiences, not being pleased by the woman they are committed to. Women have everything they need to become any fantasy he can imagine. Women must walk and carry themselves with swagger and confidence in their ability to please their spouses in any way they can imagine. I can bear witness that I do not want or need anyone else. My wife and I take time in studying one another to fulfill our desires, temptations and fantasies. We speak to one another very candidly about what turns us on. The conversation about turn-ons is interesting because it has constantly evolved over the time we have been together. There has not been a woman that has crossed my path that has made me think I needed her to fulfill me sexually. My wife knows me; I take delight in being able to come home to her. We are committed to turning one another out as often as we can. This is not a prideful statement; it should be the mindset of everyone committed to their spouse. In any way you can think regarding sex, communication, romance, affirmation, respect, loyalty and admiration, you should seek to take your spouse to ecstasy in every area of their life and emotions.

Cogito ergo sum is a Latin phrase that means "I think, therefore I am." In regard to love, how you think has everything to do with how you respond and are perceived by others. Although physical attraction may gain a man's attention, it is not enough to keep him. A woman must have depth beyond her physical presentation. What can be offered through conversation, perspective and one's ability to create solutions can be very valuable in relationships. I believe women are behind some of the best ideas, innovations and business of our history and our time. Real men love to be around smart, witty, knowledgeable and engaging women. A woman should never diminish who she is and what she knows to make a man feel more comfortable. A man wants to be with a woman who can contribute more than sex and money to a relationship. When men look at moving on and open the possibilities of entertaining other women, it involves how a woman thinks and expresses confidence in herself, marriage and her goals. Men do not just fall out of love with women. Men take issue with and question how they think and process information they see as valuable and vital to success in the relationship.

    Married women must understand that there are ladies waiting for an opportunity to seem more appealing than them. The competition from potential mistresses and girlfriends does not come from their appearance; making sustainable connections through conversations and mutual interest causes husbands to stray. The greatest tool in a married woman's kit for becoming a girlfriend and mistress is access. A married woman has access to her husband and an opportunity to blow his mind more than any other woman. Take advantage of the time and access afforded to keep your husband panting for more attention from you and no one else. A married woman is actually in competition with herself to become better than the day before. Do what you can to destroy the sliver of hope other women have in looking for a foothold into the consciousness of your husband. It's sad when a married man chooses to cheat with a woman who is actually just like his spouse. Take a moment to let that sink in.

Five

Becoming a Safe Space

I strongly believe everyone needs an outlet, a place where they can vent, blow off steam and genuinely enjoy themselves apart from the cares of the world. I also believe one's outlet is not always a place; it can also be a person. There are two types of outlets: one that is desired and one that is a necessity. It's amazing to me that mistresses always seem to know intricate details of business deals, governments, and their lovers' relationships. There is a comfort that comes with dealing with a mistress that causes a man to share things he is not willing to share with anyone else. A mistress understands that she is a place of pleasure without restrictions; there is no judgment, and she does not make an attempt to attach her issues to those of her lover. One of the biggest issues with outlets is one's mindset on fulfillment; one will gravitate toward the place or person that will give the greatest fulfillment with the least amount of resistance. Even if there are calculated risks, the punishment, in their eyes, is worth the reward. In marriage, you must learn how to become the outlet your spouse needs and wants, both fulfilling and pleasurable.

Men are not great communicators because there are not always the perfect conditions and opportunity for communication to occur. Participating in or watching sporting events involves very little conversation, but it involves a reaction. There is usually a reward and/or payoff for their participation. Whether it is their favorite team winning or receiving the spoils of victory from fishing and even enjoying the solitude of not having to deal with a nagging wife, men like outlets where they can control the outcome or do not face judgment for enjoying it.

Sports and videogames are two of my favorite outlets; both help me escape the realities of life. Even though these escapes are fleeting, they helped me become a better spouse and more attentive. I remember a period of taking out my frustration on a particular videogame. During that season of my life, I had the best scores because I was determined to release every bit of aggression on the game instead of my family. I was disappointed with my life, my income, and not being where I thought I would be professionally. Videogames helped validate me. While playing videogames, I could be a success, figure out challenges and best my peers by applying what I knew. While playing videogames, I felt I could be all of the things I struggled with in real life because I could progress at my own pace and not be limited by anything or anyone. But I met opposition from my wife, who did not understand why I needed time to "play a game" instead of being focused on spending time with her and, eventually, my kids. It took me about two years, but I eventually got the nerve to patiently explain to my wife what I was going through. She understood and didn't bother me about it. My wife shifted her focus until I did not need to be fulfilled and validated by being successful at playing videogames. I still play from time to time, but it's only to spend time with my children. Why did my interest in videogames diminish? My wife took time to learn to become everything the videogames were; she became my place of refuge, release, validation and honor. My wife took the time to understand how to be my safe place by understanding what I needed to process, communicate and deal with the issues and concerns in life.

The success of my wife came from her ability to allow me to communicate completely. I want to take a quick moment to give insight into what I mean by completely. My wife let me get everything off of my chest without interruption or judgment and with undivided attention. She was masterful in giving me a blank slate to express myself without criticizing me if my newly communicated challenges were connected to something else. Although men do not communicate it, we want to bear our souls. In sharing my feelings and emotions, I usually talked my way into a solution or saw how I was looking at the situation wrong. Having this space was important because, unlike with my videogames outlet, I was actually finding solutions instead of just blowing off steam. In the process, I came to value and appreciate my wife even more because she was helping improve my mental health and quality of life. My wife's process was simple yet stressful at times for her. She admitted that she wanted to jump in and comment, but realized her remarks and questions were not relevant until I asked for her opinion and suggestions. At that point, she knew I was ready to receive her insight and opinions. My wife gave me a pass, in a sense. In communicating with her, she understood I wasn't perfect and knew I might have a hand in my own frustration. In understanding this, she knew when and how to communicate when I was wrong in looking at a situation. At times she would tell me I needed to apologize to an individual because I was actually wrong. It is important for a man to have honest and accountable feedback. Men like having their egos stroked, but there is nothing more refreshing than a woman who knows how to communicate truth in a way that is not offensive or challenges their manhood. My wife never gives me attitude; she always gives me a solid dose of reality, whether it's good, bad or indifferent. From the time we met and began dating, she has always been genius with helping me come up with plans and strategies to overcome the challenges in my life. From budgeting and self-esteem to raising our children, my wife has always been valuable in providing wisdom in difficult situations. For some women, this is a lost art. Some women find creative ways to complain about what their spouses are not doing or complaining about what can be lost while their husbands are dealing with their issues. A man will always respect and appreciate a woman who takes time to find solutions without condemning him for simply being human. I want to make this very clear: being a safe space is not about accepting the flaws of an individual; it involves becoming a launching pad for their improvement through practical interactions that push them toward improvement instead of concealing and overlooking issues.

Becoming a wife, girlfriend and mistress is very important. As a wife, the mistress and girlfriend roles are very important in being a safe space. Men want to be heard, and if a spouse's judgment is too critical, they will seek the space in another woman. Wives must always take the stance of being an emotional stabilizer for their husbands by giving them space to share their hearts, voice and emotions. I know men who started affairs because a woman was a good listener. Eventually, the conversations became more intimate, and a sexual relationship began. These men felt drawn and compelled because the women listened to them and gave great advice. It is important to remember that mistresses and girlfriends typically care more about the quality of activity and time. In doing so, some men consider them easier to relate to. This same posture needs to be taken by wives who want to win their husbands' affection, attention and admiration. Men want to know that their wives will still love them after they share their struggles, not regret that they opened their mouths to share their truth. Men have a myriad of issues, but they tend to stem from rejection, pride, ego, greed and self-esteem. If a woman can help a man move beyond these challenges through encouraging maturity and responsibility, she is on the path to building becoming irreplaceable in his eyes. There isn't much that upsets men, but the challenges that exist can knock us off our game. Getting over the challenges in life is much easier for a man when he knows he has a woman who understands him and how to encourage him through those challenges.

How to Overcome Fear & Temptation

"It's over." This is the thought that crosses the minds of some men as the vows are spoken, and they have kissed their brides. Instead of focusing on a promising future with their new brides, selfishness creeps in and tells these men everything they cannot have or must give up. Instead of a vessel that was designed to propel a man into his destiny, he sees marriage as a hindrance to his progress and independence. The ball and chain was once an instrument to imprison, punish, and remind people of their condition as a result of unlawful behavior. A ball-and-chain mentality leads to resentment and hatred and provides an invalid excuse for infidelity. So how do we free ourselves from the ball-and-chain mentality? It really begins with men and how they feel about their spouses. Normally men choose their wives. If a man feels he has a ball and chain attached to him, it's his own fault. Men have to look at the future and what marriage means in regard to their future goals and desires. A man must consider that his wife must be a part of his goals and dreams. Sadly, compromise enters a man's heart and mind, and attributes such as a woman's appearance, sex, and a desire to have kids overwhelm long-term and short-term goals. In the same vein, a woman does not have to accept the marriage proposal if the man does not and cannot take her to the next level. As much as men want to make women happy and women want the fulfillment of getting engaged and potentially married, it is not worth the time and money unless there is compatibility and forward thinking from both parties.

Once you are married, you have to define your marriage. Your marriage can be sand, or it can be brick. Sand is easily moved and erodes when a storm and rain come. Sand can easily be manipulated and moved into another vessel. Sand can also be easily scattered. Bricks are usually cut with certain specifications and are built to withstand punishment of every kind. Brick, once set on a strong foundation, is unmovable. Even if the foundation is improperly set, the brick will not be destroyed, though it may show signs of cracking. Sand cannot withstand heat. Sand is usually melted down to make glass, a material that is easily broken and shattered. Bricks, on the other hand, need heat in their processes of creation to become strong and to mold into the expected contents. When exposed to fire, bricks keep their shape and form. To destroy a brick, it takes an outside force that puts pressure on the mortar that binds a brick to another brick. No matter how your marriage was created, whether it was made of brick or sand, it is possible to face destruction. Do not let external factors determine whether your marriage will stand. Look your spouse in the eye and imagine what your life would be without him or her. Imagine the strength that can come from the lessons learned from a difficult situation. Many people want to believe they are strong, but they are unwilling to travail through an experience to prove it. Even in its strongest state, marriage can be fragile. Although I have been divorced, I am against divorce, with the exception of the threat of bodily harm and spousal or child abuse. I carry the same sentiment about habitual cheating. If someone is habitually stepping out, they are not exhibiting regard for the health and physical well-being of themselves or their spouse. I believe all other situations can be worked out.

From counseling others, I have found the following truth about seeking attention: it starts small. Locking eyes, a hug that lingers longer than it should, lunch that turns to dinner that turns to a torrid night in the arms of a stranger we thought was familiar until we came to our senses. Married couples have to be willing to fight to keep what they have and live with a reality of hope but understand the lures and negative influences in the world. Married couples have to make romance and love real in their everyday existence. I believe couples struggle with love and its themes because they are overwhelmed and overloaded with sensationalized images from Hollywood and social media. One can find oneself guilty of not being romantic enough if one doesn't purchase three dozen long-stem roses that accompany an invitation to exotic dinners where quail and duck are served instead of chicken. Not everyone is skilled in singing, writing love letters or poetry, but I encourage everyone to start small. Build up the emotional bank of your spouse with appreciation. Simply saying thank you, the right way, can be very attractive and alluring to your spouse. Is money an issue? Polite gestures can be enough and will not cost a thing. Learn to dream again with your spouse; it does not cost a dime.

Marriages can experience traumatic episodes that can rattle the very fabric of our belief systems. No matter what, a couple can guarantee that a marriage will experience challenges. Regardless of the challenges that arise, the vows must be remembered and kept in front of us. In dealing with our spouses, and even for those who are reading this text, including those who are single and engaged, we have to watch our emotions. Emotions are dangerous if they are not properly checked. Some people are trapped with the dream of marriage and not willing to live the truth when the dream they thought they were having turns out to be a nightmare. People make hasty decisions and enter relationships because they are lonely. Others make relationship decisions solely based on the pressure of peers, family, and unfairly placed personal expectations.

Everyone has a map of their life when it comes to marriage and children. I can remember thinking in high school that I was going to get married when I was twenty-five, have eight to ten children and live happily ever after. This was not the case. Relationships, and especially marriage, cannot be limped into haphazardly. There are serious consequences after a divorce that can linger after a marriage. Alimony payments, child support, bankruptcy, low self-esteem, depression, and even suicidal thoughts can negatively impact how one feels about the future. I believe it is helpful for everyone to understand what they are committing to when they take wedding vows. I know some couples go through the motions of uttering the vows simply as a formality without considering what they really mean. Men and women are different. Men say what we need to get what we want; women need to hear what they want and hold us to it. Although the words we say exude commitment, it doesn't mean that we totally understand what has been promised. I have counseled many people who say, "He/she stood up in front of all those people and said the vows but still broke my heart." Again, they said their vows, but did they mean them? Sometimes we forget the words in the basic marital vows. Sometimes we are so caught up in the emotions of a moment that we forget that past all the romanticized veneer, marital vows are basic principles that are meant to hold us accountable.

I take you

"I take you" means I choose you. We have a choice in whom we marry, and the choice is two-fold as this part is expressed by both the man and woman. When we are upset with our spouse, we have to remember that we chose them. There was something about them that we fell in love with unless we married our spouse for our own selfish motives. In taking one's spouse, commit to them daily.

To have and to hold

"You are mine, and I belong to you. All of my needs are wrapped up in you." If you *have* something, it eliminates your need for something else. In other words, if you are getting everything you need from your spouse, then you have no need to seek a relationship outside of the marital relationship. Holding onto your spouse also means that you will commit to them and stay with them. If you are not getting what you need, then you must communicate it to your spouse, whether it be emotional, physical or spiritual. Marriage is beautiful when the relationship is committed and open to improvement through working together. To have and to hold also says, "I am in this with you for the long haul."

For better or for worse

This is self-explanatory. The only issue is that people do not know how bad things may become. A bad situation does not mean the end of a marriage; it means you have an opportunity to come together to make the solutions that will change your fate. When I face a challenging situation, my wife and I rehearse our past victories in difficult situations and strategize to overcome the challenges of life. Things can always be better, but when the worst of life rears its head, this is when spouses should come together and fight to experience the best of life once again.

For richer, for poorer

Some people say that the love of money is the root of all evil, but I would say it is also the demise of good marriages. Do not measure the success of your marriage by how much money you have. Many people grow up seeing what their parents have amassed over many years of hard work, but do not see their parents struggle to reach that level of financial success. Couples must not look at marriage like a struggling business in a way that one thinks they can remove "Business Steve" and acquire "Business Mike" and have a better life simply because he makes more money. Spouses must work together in the good times and the lean times. Finances should not determine your happiness or willingness to stay committed to the marriage.

In sickness and in health

There is no reason to walk away from a spouse in a time of need. Illness does not give anyone a reason to disregard marital responsibilities. This is a time when your spouse has the greatest needs; stick by the one you promised your life to. It is shameful to leave someone when they are in their worst state. No matter how trying or difficult an illness may be, there are brighter days on the other side of it.

To love and to cherish

Love is difficult to measure or define. I believe that love can only be measured by how much someone is willing to give up for another person while ensuring their best interest is at the forefront of their mind and heart. Men see love as something they have to master to get a woman, while it is also an expectation of a woman to keep her. For men, love is on the front end of the obligation to win a woman, but women expect men to continue to show its evidence long after the first utterance of the word. Love should never be measured by words, but by the action and work that follow. How much are you willing to sacrifice to make another's dream come true? How much time are you willing to give up? How much money do you plan to invest in their future? I did not say, "How much are you willing to spend on them?" This is not love. An investment denotes a long-term commitment; simply spending money is wasteful and creates bitterness because the rate of return is less. Love should not involve emotions. Emotions cause us to make irrational decisions. Emotions are likened to reality television. You see something that seems to be real, but is stylized to capture a particular moment, and once the truth comes out, reality television has you wondering what happened in between episodes. Love is more eternal and true. You know exactly what you are getting; you know what the highs and lows are, and you are consistently fulfilled versus waiting for a special moment instead of living a special life with someone.

Until death do us part

This is where the rubber meets the road. Being in a military town, I have come to know young women who become widows because their husbands were killed in combat. Death is the clincher in marriage. Do not give yourself a way out. Instead, find every reason you can to work diligently on perfecting and improving your marriage. Even if people tell you it's over, you have the power and authority to determine when your marriage is final. If there is abuse in the marriage or habits that are detrimental to your health and well-being, use common sense to ensure your safety. Sometimes the death is not a physical death. One can tap out and exhibit behavior that denotes their unwillingness to connect. Weigh all of your options; choose to work hard until you have exhausted all of your possibilities.

How can men and women work together to make sure each other is taken care of? The ultimate choice is up to you, the reader of this text. I have taken considerable time and consideration to give sound advice. No matter what happens from here, remember that forgiveness is the key. If you are someone who likes to quip, "I'll forgive, but I won't forget," then you need to forget the wrongs that caused you to slip into bitterness and hatred.

Seven

Epilogue: The Power of Choice

Everything written in this book is born of honesty and experience from my personal encounters with the choices I made and decided not to make about marriage. I speak, at times, about my wife, Tanesha, in this book. I love her dearly and have learned so much from our relationship. I want to continue my honesty now and discuss my ex-wife. What I am about to share is not to cast a negative light; it's to bring clarity and context to what I shared previously. It is from my experience with my ex-wife that I hope to give insight into what can cause a relationship and marriage to fail.

My ex-wife was a woman I loved unconditionally. I was infatuated with her and devoted my life to making her happy. If my ex-wife wanted anything, I would move heaven and earth for her. I served her at every turn and never questioned her. I honestly thought if I made her happy, that she, in turn, would make me happy. Slowly, our relationship eroded into a one-sided event. I lost myself and dug deeper holes personally because I did not express what I wanted or needed from her and our relationship. I did not consider the negative effects of my behavior and mindset; I was prone to manipulation and did not realize it.

Eventually, I found myself under pressure, and the relationship went from being fun to helpless expectations. She wanted to get married. At the time, I was a recent college graduate, and she was six years older than me. We dated for seven months and when she didn't get a ring for her birthday, every conversation was driven by marriage and my intentions with her. Threats and ultimatums followed. The threat I liked the least was, "I'm going to send you back home to your mom if I'm not married soon." Since I liked her and did not want to move back home with my mom, I asked her to marry me. She agreed, but used sex to get me to move things along. After sex was cut off, we rushed and put together a wedding in three weeks. I thought I would be happy after the wedding, but I was miserable. I thought if I gave her everything she wanted, it would bring fulfillment to me. I thought my opinions would be heard and respected by making her my wife. Once we were married, she ignored me. I didn't feel important. We didn't have sex, and we rarely spoke. I purchased a home with my ex-wife because she wanted one. My last straw was her expressing a desire to have a baby. We weren't even having sex, so where was a baby going to come from? It was at that moment I felt I was a part of her "life checklist." I was an accessory in her life, but not a part of it. I felt I was only valuable when she bragged about how loyal I was. I felt stupid. How had I allowed this to happen to me? I realized years later that our relationship lacked balance. True love and healthy relationships are not based on what someone can do or provide. I shouldn't have given in to the thought of marrying a woman to make me happy.

The last thing I wanted in life was a divorce, but my ex-wife drove me to it, then verbally berated me for the decision I made because she refused to work on our relationship. She wanted me to stay silent, make her happy and fade into the sunset. I lost so much of myself that I wanted a fresh start. The only truth I knew was making her happy. Beyond that, I was lost; I just waited for the next instruction from her and went to work. When I realized this about myself, I was ashamed. How had I let someone control my life? I was worn down emotionally and mentally; all I ever wanted to do was make her happy, but that doesn't make a successful relationship.

Everything I discussed in this book, from the relationship detox, to understanding competition and even how men see the role of a wife, girlfriend and mistress, is real. Did I cheat on my ex-wife? Yes, in a sense. I never engaged in a sexual relationship with another woman, but I did replace my ex-wife in every other facet of our relationship. I remember one occasion when I was having an intimate conversation with another woman while my ex-wife was present. The young lady and I spoke exclusively for several hours, and my ex-wife ignored us. My ex-wife was so self-absorbed that she didn't realize that the young lady I was talking to preyed on her ignorance and lack of attention. My ex-wife thought my strict obedience to her meant I was happy with her, which was the furthest thing from the truth. Women must understand the danger of getting everything they want. In some cases, there is a tremendous price for not being realistic and balanced in pursuit of their desires.

Epilogue: The Power of Choice

On another occasion, I begged my ex-wife to slow down from being involved in the community and church activities so we could have more time together. I wanted to work on our relationship. My request fell on deaf ears. Angry with her response, I called an old flame and just popped up at her home. I knew how long my ex-wife's meeting was going to last and how long it was going to take me to get home from my old flame's house. I sat down, talked and left; my old flame was completely oblivious as to why I stopped by. Although I wanted to cheat, I didn't. I did not want to shame my marriage. I knew I wanted to leave. I also wanted to make sure I had a clear conscience when I left. Sleeping with someone would have compelled me to stay; it would have given me something to throw in her face to show her how bad things had become in my eyes. In the end, the proverbial salt in the wound would not have been worth it.

This is the first time I've mentioned these details. I never shared them with my ex-wife. I didn't feel comfortable speaking with her about this, nor did I see the need at the time. I mention these situations because one does not know what one's spouse is enduring to remain true even in tumultuous situations. Always give your spouse space to hear their concerns and sincerely respond to them if you want to keep your marriage intact.

Considering my experiences with my ex-wife played a part in this book. There are plenty of men like me who did not speak up and do not know how to speak up. Ladies, give your loved one space and opportunity to communicate with you honestly. Do not get defensive; examine yourself. No one is right all of the time; a successful relationship is not predicated on how much your spouse lets you get away with. The failure of my first marriage is completely my fault. I take full responsibility for how things transpired. Honestly, the seeds of my failed first marriage were sown while we were dating. I never took time to understand my ex-wife, learn her personality, motivations and heart. I knew my ex-wife was very successful, financially stable, known in the community, educated and attractive. I was foolish in my assessment because I learned all of these things did not matter. I was not marrying her profile; I joined myself to a woman who did things that did not measure up to who she really was.

As a realtor, I know there is always an issue somewhere with a home. It's only a matter of time before it is exposed. In my immaturity, I did not take the time to thoroughly inspect

Epilogue: The Power of Choice

my ex-wife prior to committing to her. On the other hand, I did not examine myself, either; I was not ready for marriage. I identified other people's perceptions of what made a great relationship. I depended on affirmations and compliments on how good my ex-wife and I looked together to guide my emotions and view of our relationship. Everything made sense and looked good from the eyes of others, so things must be great, right? I needed more time to develop and learn who I was beyond my issues, challenges and perceptions before I allowed someone to become a part of my existence that was built on rejection, low self-esteem and pride.

I sincerely want my truth to free others. When one makes a choice for honest self-examination with the appropriate action to correct their wrongs, it is one of the most liberating experiences in one's life. In the end, I am not proud of the failure of my first marriage. I called and apologized to my ex-wife for my failures as a man and how I handled everything with her. I still want the best for her; I wish her well in her future endeavors.

The last choice I made in regard to personal relationships was the best one. After divorcing my ex-wife, I made a decision to throw away the idea of marriage for at least 15 to 20 years. If I did get married, it would be to whomever I was with at the time – nothing special. I figured at that point in my life, I would want someone who would be a great travel companion and someone to grow old with.

On a night in 2005, I met my wife, Tanesha. I did everything I could to fight the urge to simply speak to her. My life was a mess, and I really did not want to get rejected by another woman. But I spoke, and my conversation with her was the best I ever experienced with the opposite sex. I felt a connection with her; the connection wasn't sexual or emotional. I understood her, and she understood me. We dated for two years, and the first year was rough. It took some time, but we both worked through our challenges and committed to being in a relationship with each other. The second year was full of peace, love, mutual respect and ultimately ended with our marriage. With Tanesha, I made a choice to let go of all the fear and hang-ups I had. I chose to love Tanesha unconditionally without the lens of my past experiences driving how I treated her and related to her. There comes a time when past hurt, frustration and pain are not defense mechanisms but foolish

Epilogue: The Power of Choice

barriers that keep us from experiencing true happiness and fulfillment.

I will never forget the day and time Tanesha came into my life. Once I let go of pain and disappointment, I was able to live a life of truth and respect. It is my sincerest hope, desire and prayer that you are able to do so as well. Ultimately, I had to forgive myself. I had to rebuild trust in myself to make good decisions. For some time, I believed I deserved some of the bad things going on in my life because of my decision-making process. This is far from the truth; we all must come to a place of accountability. On the other side of taking responsibility for our missteps in life, we all can have a better quality of life. I sincerely hope your marriage is improved by the lessons I've learned and shared in this book.

www.ingramcontent.com/pod-product-compliance
Lightning Source LLC
LaVergne TN
LVHW021614080426
835510LV00019B/2573